In keeping with literary tradition, we would have liked
to dedicate this book to our moms. However, in the first section alone
are the words "nipples," "breasts," "balls," "bitch," "shit," "nuts,"
"pussy," "genitals," "man-boobs," and "go fuck yourself,"
so we decided to spare everyone the overwhelming discomfort.

SPORTS & FITNESS

Guys who insist on playing everything shirts & skins............................11
Guys who are more comfortable nude at the gym than I am at home ...13
Guys who verbally encourage themselves while working out...............17
Obese guys who lose to skinny guys in eating competitions.................19
Guys who know more about sports than we wish they did 23
Guys who work out with their girlfriends..25
Guys who know karate who've never kicked anyone's ass 27
Guys who still wonder how much we can bench 29
Guys who are way too into their company softball team 31
Guys in steam rooms with wandering eyes...35
Guy gym trainers with terrible bodies..37
Guys who bring their own pool sticks to bars 39

SEX & RELATIONSHIPS

Guys who say, "We're pregnant" 43
Oblivious third-wheel guys 45
Picky wingmen 47
Guys who keep reminding us of the time they had a threesome...........49
Guys who insist a stripper was into them 51

DON'T BE THAT GUY

A COLLECTION OF 60 ANNOYING GUYS WE ALL KNOW AND WISH WE DIDN'T

Written by Colin Nissan
Illustrated by Sean Farrell

THREE RIVERS PRESS
NEW YORK

All rights reserved.
Published in the United States by Three Rivers Press,
an imprint of the Crown Publishing Group,
a division of Random House, Inc., New York.
www.crownpublishing.com

Three Rivers Press and the Tugboat design are registered
trademarks of Random House, Inc.

Library of Congress Cataloging-in-Publication Data
is available upon request.

ISBN 978-0-307-45036-4

Printed in the United States of America

10 9 8 7 6 5 4 3 2 1

First Edition

Guys who propose to their girlfriends in hot air balloons 55
Guys who tell us how many times they beat off last night 57
Guys who include hookers in their lifetime tally of lays 59
Guys in pornos who don't wear condoms 61
Guys who wear T-shirts declaring their prowess with the
female anatomy 65
Incredibly gay guys who are the last ones to know it..................69
Guys who email us porn that haunts our dreams 71

GROOMING, HYGIENE & FASHION

Guys with Amish beards who aren't Amish.............................75
Guys with startling unibrows...81
Guys getting manicures in broad daylight.............................83
Guys with perfect perma-scruff 85
Guys who can't stop pitting..87
Guys who shave their balls...91
Balding guys who haven't shaved their heads yet.....................93
Guys who go to costume parties dressed as anything adorable 95
Guys who wear vintage clothes 99
Guys who wear winter hats indoors...................................101

ETIQUETTE

Guys who over-hug...107
Guys who won't acknowledge their lactose intolerance................111
Guys who strike up conversations at urinals 113
Practical joke guys who mistake danger for humor 117
Guys who try to get us to look at their giant turds.................119
Guys who think we have a special handshake when we really don't..121
Guys who rub their friends' shoulders...............................123
Old guys who fart and think we don't notice 125
Guys who bring more than one other guy to a party 127

Guys who actually think they do a good robot 129

Guys who try to get us to bet on everything 131

Guys who explode in public bathrooms 133

Guys who wear sunglasses during nonprofessional poker games 135

BARS, DRINKING & ENTERTAINMENT

Guys who try to turn every activity into a drinking activity 139

Guys in bars who pretend they're reading.............................141

Guys who pretend they're having a lot more fun than they
really are 143

Guys who dodge paying for their round of drinks 145

Guys who impersonate Arnold Schwarzenegger 147

A-holes who work the doors at clubs.................................151

Guys in Vegas who insist on gambling despite being plastered..........153

Barbacks who stand around while we need drinks 155

Guys who still quote *The Holy Grail* and/or *Spinal Tap*...............157

Guys who always have a new shitty band for us to listen to 161

Guys who listen to Dave Matthews on purpose 163

Guys who dance with the girls dancing on the bar....................167

FINAL EXAM

The Don't Be That Guy Quiz 169

FOREWORD

Don't Be That Guy is for anyone who's ever looked across the room and said, "Is it me, or is that guy a complete ass?" In these pages you'll find validation that he is, in fact, a complete ass, and feel justified in pointing and laughing at him.

You'll also gain a better understanding of the friends, colleagues, boyfriends, brothers, and husbands in your lives—while dramatically improving your ability to mock them.

This book is also for the guys themselves. The ones who make us shake our heads at all the annoying little things they do. To all of you, consider this book a friendly full-length mirror: an honest little reflection to help you see the bonehead we all see in you.

Now, there is one caution worth mentioning before you get started. You may find yourself reading along and chuckling at the ironic truth of these insights, when suddenly the laughter stops.

You turn the page and see something that isn't funny at all: you.

This can happen unexpectedly, and can hurt a little. But don't be alarmed, there's a whole new guy to ridicule on the next page. If, however, it's you again . . . well, apparently you've got some stuff to sort out.

SPORTS
&
FITNESS

★ DON'T BE THAT GUY ★

GUYS WHO INSIST ON PLAYING EVERYTHING SHIRTS & SKINS

We get it. You're very attractive. Your chest and abs are well-defined. Your skin is tanned and, dare I say, supple.

It must be nice to live in your world, actually looking forward to opportunities to unveil your Aryan genealogy.

We, on the other hand, are pear-shaped. We have bacne, outee belly buttons, and weird nipples.

Our bodies aren't something we're eager to showcase. In fact, it wasn't long ago that we became comfortable swimming shirtless.

So let's all just take a moment to memorize our teammates' faces. There are only five of us; it shouldn't be too hard.

GUYS WHO ARE MORE COMFORTABLE NUDE AT THE GYM THAN I AM AT HOME

Exactly how much of a hindrance would a towel around your waist be while you shave or clean your ears?

Even when you weigh yourself, couldn't you just deduct a pound to account for the extra weight?

I think you could.

It seems you've found yourself a nice little loophole in the anti-exhibitionism laws of our great country.

Good for you, nude gym guy.

And pretty freaking awful for us.

SOME NAKED LOCKER ROOM **CLASSICS**

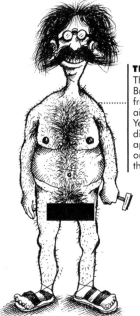

THE PROFESSOR
This guy has a Wilfred Brimley mustache, yellowed from years of dank library air, pipe smoke, and oatmeal. Yet as unappealing as that dingy lip caterpillar is, you appreciate it for being the only skin on his pasty body that isn't exposed.

THE SAGGER
This guy has balls that sag like a stork carrying twins in a blanket. His aged breasts hang off his chest like half-empty hot water bottles. He is a skeleton wearing a human suit two sizes too big, and yet he still possesses the remarkable confidence to shave naked.

THE WOOKIE
This guy is a haunting optical illusion. On first glance, you feel your eyes pass over a clothed man. Upon further examination, however, you realize those aren't normal clothes he's wearing. Those are hair clothes. And although you look away as soon as humanly possible, like the burning imprint of the sun in your eyes, his image lingers.

THE ADONIS
This guy can't get over how stunning he is. We see it in the way he steals glances of his reflection in the mirror, and in the tenderness with which he moisturizes every square inch of his Romanesque physique. And as he gathers his belongings to go home, we're left to imagine the ravenous love-making session he will have with himself when he gets there.

★ DON'T BE THAT GUY ★

GUYS WHO VERBALLY ENCOURAGE THEMSELVES WHILE WORKING OUT

It's always great to see a guy offering up friendly encouragement at the gym.

Except when it's to himself.

An under-your-breath rep count is perfectly understandable, but here's what we don't want to hear:

"Come on Jimmy, come on buddy, pump that shit, that's it, fuckin' pump it, bitch! You feel that burn? You feel that shit? Yeah you do Jimmy! Yeah you do!!"

The funny thing is, this self-pep talk would work just as well if you think it. . . .

But it's not about that, is it, Jimmy?

★ DON'T BE THAT GUY ★

OBESE GUYS WHO LOSE TO SKINNY GUYS IN EATING COMPETITIONS

While there are very few benefits to being plus-sized, there are fleeting moments of grandeur.

Like when you're sitting next to an eighty-five-pound Japanese kid at a hot-dog-eating contest.

There isn't an anatomical or psychological reason for you to lose here.

You should win, then eat him—partly to send a message, and partly because you could still use a little something.

So unless you want all those hours at Sizzler to be in vain, I suggest you start shoveling some weenies down your throat.

Anatomy of a Competitive Eater

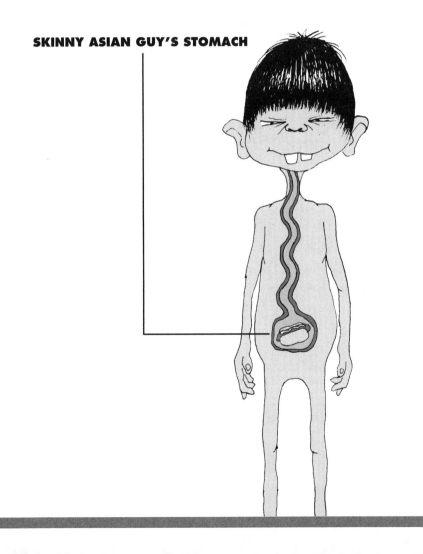

SKINNY ASIAN GUY'S STOMACH

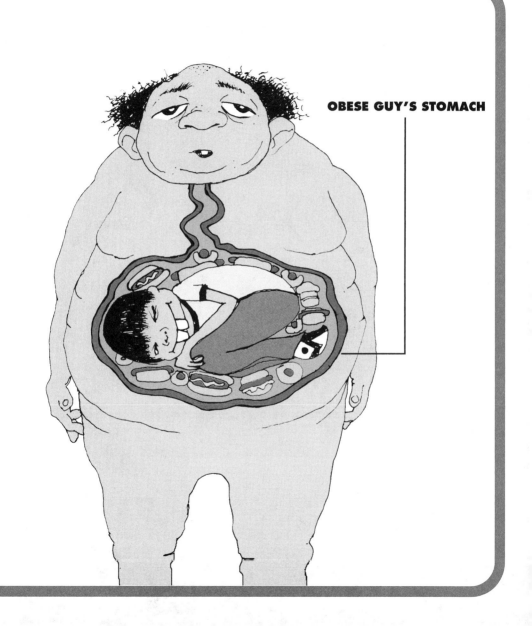

OBESE GUY'S STOMACH

★ DON'T BE THAT GUY ★

GUYS WHO KNOW MORE ABOUT SPORTS THAN WE WISH THEY DID

Your ability to retain such a wealth of information is truly amazing. Your inability to shut your pie-hole, however, is infuriating.

No one asked how many triple-doubles LeBron had last season.

No one asked how many touchdowns Manning threw for in 2004.

But you still tell us. And tell us.

Hey, in the spirit of sports trivia questions, here's one for you:

Who's about to get a right uppercut to the nuts?

★ DON'T BE THAT GUY ★

GUYS WHO WORK OUT WITH THEIR GIRLFRIENDS

Aren't you just capital "A" adorable, as you struggle through the most impractical exercise partnership on the planet?

Hauling those forty-five-pound plates on and off the bar every two minutes.

Constantly readjusting each machine to account for your twelve-inch height difference.

It's a lot of work.

Not only that, but you and Cuddlebums are on a very short road to Stifleville.

Living, eating, and sleeping together are just about all most relationships can handle.

★ DON'T BE THAT GUY ★

GUYS WHO KNOW KARATE WHO'VE NEVER KICKED ANYONE'S ASS

In all the years since we've known you, we haven't seen you punch a single person, let alone brush someone off with one of those roundhouse kicks we've been hearing so much about.

All we ever see you do is stretch out. And reason with people.

It's upsetting.

We'd like to believe you're bound by some ancient code of honor because of your unfair advantage over opponents. But odds are leaning toward you just being a huge pussy.

You paid good money to learn how to tear someone's larynx out of his throat. Frankly, it's troubling to watch you squander it.

At the very least, it wouldn't kill you to break a frigging board in half for us.

★ DON'T BE THAT GUY ★

GUYS WHO STILL WONDER HOW MUCH WE CAN BENCH

Take a good look at my body.

I haven't picked up a free weight in about ten years, and I'm pretty sure you haven't either.

This isn't something you should be even remotely curious about anymore. But you are.

I know I'm in for it every time the topic of exercise comes up—you get that weird look in your eye, then you scan my torso, make that little head nod at me, and out it comes.

I promise if I stop doing water aerobics and start maxing out again, I'll let you know how I do.

GUYS WHO ARE WAY TOO INTO THEIR COMPANY SOFTBALL TEAM

Let me guess . . . you were a scouted high school player and would have gotten that scholarship if you hadn't torn your ACL in the division playoffs?

Well, a couple of things have changed since then, like you being a middle-aged accountant now.

The scouts are long gone, I'm afraid, so you can stop double-gunning the other accountants and try to enjoy your very uncompetitive game of softball.

The rest of us are here for one very specific reason: free beer at the post-game bar. And the sooner you stop arguing with the volunteer ump, the sooner we can make that happen.

A QUIZ
FOR THE UNNECESSARILY COMPETITIVE MIDDLE-AGED CORPORATE ATHLETE

If you answer yes to any of these,
it's time to take things down a couple of notches.

1) **Do you limber up the day of the game in the presence of coworkers?**
   ○ NO   ○ YES

2) **Do you own cleats?**
   ○ NO   ○ YES

3) **Do you wear the game shirt for all or any part of the workday?**
   ○ NO   ○ YES

4) **Does the fact that no one else owns batting gloves disgust you?**
   ○ NO   ○ YES

5) **Do you send company-wide emails the day after the game entitled: "RE: Disappointed doesn't begin to describe how I feel about all of you this morning"?**
   ○ NO   ○ YES

6) **Have you tried, on numerous occasions, to get everyone to pitch in for official MLB bases?**
   ○ NO   ○ YES

7) **Has a colleague told you to "go fuck yourself" after you tried to cut him from the team?**
   ○ NO   ○ YES

8) **Do you prominently display the MVP trophy that you awarded yourself in your cubicle?**
   ○ NO   ○ YES

9) **Have you made Leslie from accounts receivable cry?**
   ○ NO   ○ YES

★ DON'T BE THAT GUY ★

GUYS IN STEAM ROOMS WITH WANDERING EYES

Besides loosening our muscles, this steam is serving another very important purpose.

It's keeping us from seeing each other's genitals.

So when the steam cloud lifts between surges, and the faint, hazy images of our wee-wees become all too clear, please keep your head down.

In a few moments, the haze will be back and order will once again be restored.

★ DON'T BE THAT GUY ★

GUY GYM TRAINERS WITH TERRIBLE BODIES

You know when you're encouraging me to battle through one more crunch, and I hesitate?

It's not because I'm tired. It's because I'm staring at your enormous spare tire wondering why the hell I'm taking exercise advice from Grimace.

Give me one good reason why I shouldn't do the exact opposite of what you tell me.

Because as it stands now with your man-boobs dangling in my face, I'm not feeling it.

★ DON'T BE THAT GUY ★

GUYS WHO BRING THEIR OWN POOL STICKS TO BARS

There's really only one thing to say here:

You better be fucking amazing at pool.

I'm not talking beat-your-friends amazing, I'm talking trick-shots-with-flaming-rings amazing.

Honestly, what do you think we're thinking while you screw that thing together and chalk up your hands?

I'll tell you: "Please, Lord, let him rip the felt on his break."

Something possessed you to leave your house carrying a long, leather-sheathed case.

For your sake, I hope it's talent.

RELATIONSHIPS

★ DON'T BE THAT GUY ★

GUYS WHO SAY, "WE'RE PREGNANT"

This is no different than you getting kicked in the nuts and your wife telling everyone, "We just got kicked in the nuts," while you're curled up on the ground.

Even though you think she likes hearing you say "we," deep down she resents it.

Why?

Maybe it's because she's the one who'll be passing a human through her tiny vagina, and you're the one who'll be standing next to her eating Twizzlers.

So remember, your wife's the one who's pregnant.

You're just the one who did it to her.

★ DON'T BE THAT GUY ★

OBLIVIOUS THIRD-WHEEL GUYS

No matter how witty and fascinating your yarns may be, the inevitable fact remains that you're not getting any tonight.

It's far too late to turn this ship around. You went from wingman to creepy guy about two hours ago.

So please, make this beer your last and let your friend get it on before the sun comes up.

In the event you're actually holding out for a threesome, the following graphic illustrates the likelihood of this occurring.

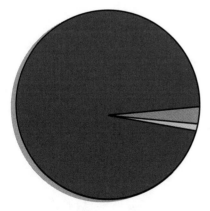

99.65% Your friend will hook up

0.33% An ostrich with your mom riding it will run through your living room

0.02% Threesome

★ DON'T BE THAT GUY ★

PICKY WINGMEN

By definition, a wingman is a guy who keeps another girl occupied while his friend makes his move.

Also by definition, you don't get to choose who you keep occupied.

Sometimes it works out nicely for you too, and that's a fun little bonus.

Other times, she'll have a mullet and arm hair like Robin Williams.

And that's okay, because tonight your needs are secondary. So bat those eyelashes and get to work.

★ DON'T BE THAT GUY ★

GUYS WHO KEEP REMINDING US OF THE TIME THEY HAD A THREESOME

We were happy for you the first time you told us this story eight years ago, but now we want to choke you every time you find an excuse to bring it up.

The Three Amigos comes on cable and whammo, we're listening to how you couldn't tell whose legs were whose that night because it was so "crazy."

Perhaps you don't feel like you've rubbed it in properly, but I can assure you that you have.

You crossed a line that we will never cross.

Now please let us enjoy our stupid single-partner sex in peace.

★ DON'T BE THAT GUY ★

GUYS WHO INSIST A STRIPPER WAS INTO THEM

Why do you insist on putting us through the same painful speech every time we leave a strip club?

"You guys, this time was totally different, I swear, I'm telling you it was weird, this girl gave me like two free dances and was totally giving me the vibe. . . ."

First off, everything you say until your raging hard-on disappears is in question, but let's go ahead and break this down anyway. While it was, in fact, noteworthy that she gave you two free dances, let's not forget that you paid for seventeen. That, my friend, is not the mark of someone who was into you, but that of a true professional. Of course we all dream of making free, sweet love to a stripper, but the fact remains that you were too dizzied by the haze of coconut body spray to realize she was actually just doing her job. So please stop this "connection" nonsense; let's all just hit the ATM again, get some eggs, and reminisce about the fake sex we just paid for.

STRIPPER TRANSLATION GUIDE

For those who don't speak stripper, this helpful dialogue decoder will help you understand what she's actually saying, despite what you'd like to believe.

WHAT SHE'S SAYING:

You're making me so hot.

WHAT SHE'S SAYING:

Hey, I'm Amber. I'm super-horny.

WHAT SHE'S REALLY SAYING:

Your spare tire is enormous.

WHAT SHE'S REALLY SAYING:

Hey, I'm Janet. I have crabs.

★ DON'T BE THAT GUY ★

GUYS WHO PROPOSE TO THEIR GIRLFRIENDS IN HOT AIR BALLOONS

Not only is this a slap in the face to those of us making ground proposals, but you've screwed yourself in the process.

Your little aerial stunt has set the romantic-cliché bar extremely high for the remainder of your relationship.

So get ready to ride white horses on her birthday, swim with dolphins on Valentine's Day, and adopt a Laotian baby on your anniversary.

She's expecting some crazy-ass shit for the rest of your lives together, and it's all your fault.

★ DON'T BE THAT GUY ★

GUYS WHO TELL US HOW MANY TIMES THEY BEAT OFF LAST NIGHT

In the spirit of confessions, here's one for you:

I don't like it when you talk to me about masturbating.

It makes me feel weird.

Honestly, what reaction do you think you're going to get out of anyone besides nausea?

We've all had our big nights, so to speak, but some personal triumphs should remain, well, personal.

★ DON'T BE THAT GUY ★

GUYS WHO INCLUDE HOOKERS IN THEIR LIFETIME TALLY OF LAYS

Nope.

Inherent in the definition of "lay" is some semblance of conquest. Some effort on your part other than reaching into your wallet.

Even if you recall a particularly tender moment during a rendezvous with a pro, that still doesn't shift her into the "civilian sex" column.

It puts her into the "tender prostitute sex" column.

So the next time you're throwing your head back in search of a total, weed out the women you remember going to an ATM with afterward.

★ DON'T BE THAT GUY ★

GUYS IN PORNOS WHO DON'T WEAR CONDOMS

You look pretty happy for someone who's dying soon.

I don't think I need to tell you this, but you've made a terrible decision.

I'm sure you got some pressure from the director to go bareback, but let's remember this was the same man who fed you the line:

"You want some more of this pork hammer?"

So consider the source.

And now after all your hard work, you probably won't even live to see *Clit Parade 6* hit the silver screen.

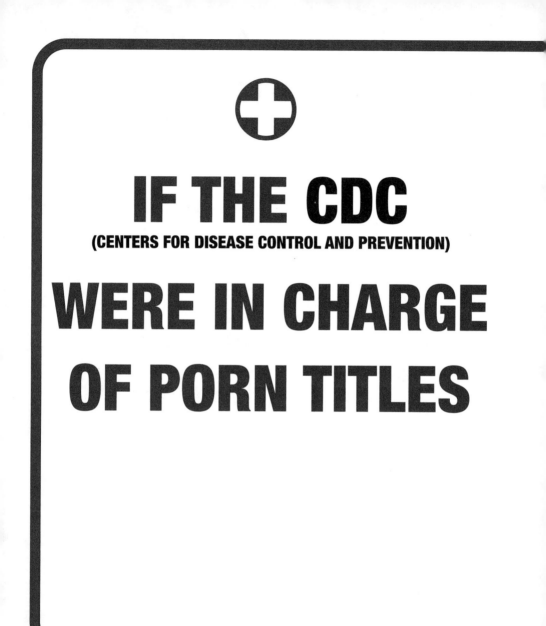

★ DON'T BE THAT GUY ★

GUYS WHO WEAR T-SHIRTS DECLARING THEIR PROWESS WITH THE FEMALE ANATOMY

Wow, you must be the "Pussy Invader." It's nice to meet you.

If only the irony of this clothing choice wasn't lost on you.

The mere fact that you wear this shirt tells us that you are an invader of nothing, least of all pussy.

Not that you should wear a "Virgin Questioning His Sexuality" shirt, but a nice blank tee from the Gap never hurt anyone.

A few more you shouldn't wear anymore:

DRINKING-RELATED

MY OTHER BODY

IS NOT

AN ALCOHOLIC

PUKING
just means
the BEER is working!

I'M THE DESIGNATED DRIVER
(Designated to get shitfaced!)

THESE ARE
PRESCRIPTION
BEER GOGGLES

★ DON'T BE THAT GUY ★

INCREDIBLY GAY GUYS WHO ARE THE LAST ONES TO KNOW IT

You have a mustache.

You make scones.

You say, "You go, girl."

You bang dudes.

This is the real thing, my friend. The real McCoy.

It's time to let yourself in on it, because everyone else already is.

Your wife and kids aren't throwing anyone off your scent, and neither is your deluxe ESPN package.

You're a very gay man.

So kick that closet door down and tell the world.

Just don't be upset when no one gasps.

★ DON'T BE THAT GUY ★

GUYS WHO EMAIL US PORN THAT HAUNTS OUR DREAMS

Your name pops up in our inbox and it can only mean one thing: we're seconds away from watching a transvestite fuck a seal.

Of course, it's ultimately our decision to watch it or not. We're adults.

We could choose not to see German twins make number two on each other.

But when it's right there, just a click away, we must.

Over the years, you have shown me things I wish I never knew existed, and robbed me of my sweet innocence in the process.

For that, sir, I will never forgive you.

GROOMING,

HYGIENE

&

Fashion

GUYS WITH AMISH BEARDS WHO AREN'T AMISH

This isn't a good look for the Amish and it certainly isn't a good look for you.

Of all the things to borrow from the residents of Lancaster County, their beard was a terrible choice.

What about their work ethic or their family values? Both admirable qualities you could have just as easily adopted.

I guess we should all be thankful you didn't go with the hats.

THE UNLIKELY YET SURPRISINGLY CHARMING FRIENDSHIP BETWEEN AN AMISH GUY and a GUY with an AMISH BEARD

"Chillin' at the Crib"

THE UNLIKELY YET SURPRISINGLY CHARMING FRIENDSHIP BETWEEN AN AMISH GUY and a GUY with an AMISH BEARD

"Road Trip"

★ DON'T BE THAT GUY ★

GUYS WITH STARTLING UNIBROWS

Your priorities are beyond mere physical appearance and I respect that. But it's time to reprioritize and get that crazy thing off your face.

This isn't a few connecting hairs you're dealing with, this is a full-blown Bert and Ernie catastrophe.

You have to be tired of people's eye contact slipping away during conversations, drifting upward, locking in on your browpillar.

The day has come, my swarthy friend, to restore that vital strip of skin real estate, and your dignity in the process.

★ DON'T BE THAT GUY ★

GUYS GETTING MANICURES IN BROAD DAYLIGHT

You see me . . . I know you see me.

Yoo-hoo . . . right here in the window. Look at me.

Look up from your nail treatment and look at me.

This is bad.

What you're doing is very bad. Very shameful.

You know how I know?

Because you won't look at me.

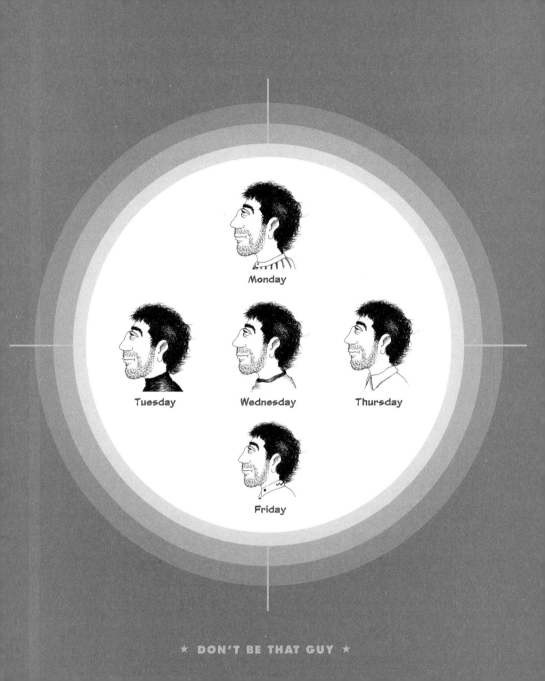

Monday

Tuesday   Wednesday   Thursday

Friday

GUYS WITH PERFECT PERMA-SCRUFF

Man, it looks like you just didn't have a chance to shave the last couple of days, huh? It's been rough with all the late nights and threesomes, right?

Wrong.

You, sir, have labored over this scruff. You have carefully sculpted it. Contoured it. Groomed it to look like you don't care, when in fact you do care.

You care very much.

You've put way more time into this Wham! look than a guy who actually shaves every morning.

So while you're looking off into space, rubbing your bristly chin, just know that we know.

★ DON'T BE THAT GUY ★

GUYS WHO CAN'T STOP PITTING

There's an entire aisle in the drugstore devoted to armpits.

Surely there's some combination of products to stop those two Rorschach blots from seeping through both of your shirts.

I'm not picking on your hormones—clearly your pH balance is out of whack.

But please do us the favor of pursuing a cure.

You owe us that.

And in the meantime, we'll do our best to maintain eye contact with you when you lift up your arms.

THE PIT STAIN ACCEPTABILITY CHART

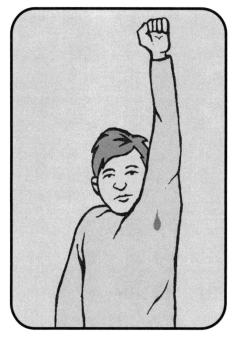

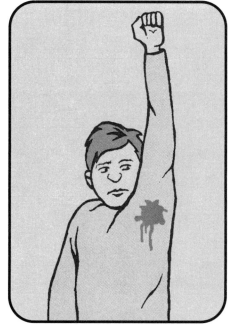

THE TEAR DROP

Acceptable when you're giving a presentation at work and realize that your slides are out of order.

THE MELTED ICE CUBE

Acceptable when you're hooking up with a girl you met in a dark bar and she has a huge dick.

THE WATER BALLOON

Acceptable when you're driving home on a rainy night and hit a deer but keep driving, refusing to acknowledge the fact that the deer didn't have antlers or four legs and that he was carrying a big backpack and screamed "Fuuuuuuck!" right before you hit him.

THE SHAMU

Acceptable when you're in the front row at Sea World.

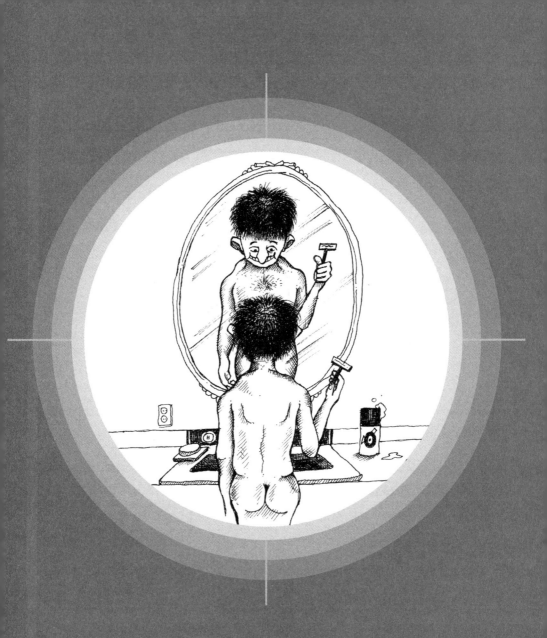

★ DON'T BE THAT GUY ★

GUYS WHO SHAVE THEIR BALLS

There is one thing I can assure you of with the utmost confidence: your balls are not even a little bit more attractive after you shave them.

You could paint little hearts all over them and dip them in glitter and they'd still be the ugliest part of the human anatomy.

Bringing a blade near them could very well be the most pointless and hazardous expression of vanity since the Chinese invented foot binding.

Trust me, in the end no girl is going to think, "Mmm, look how smooth that guy's balls are."

She's going to think, "Eww, balls. Eww, shaved balls."

★ DON'T BE THAT GUY ★

BALDING GUYS WHO HAVEN'T SHAVED THEIR HEADS YET

You're really missing an enormous opportunity to not look terrible anymore.

Fate is throwing you a huge bone here. For probably the first time ever, the bald look is actually in fashion, yet for some reason you insist on this clownlike homage to the 1970s.

Think about it, just five minutes with a pair of clippers could silence the laughter—and maybe even get you back into the dating pool for another go at it.

GUYS WHO GO TO COSTUME PARTIES DRESSED AS ANYTHING ADORABLE

This is very simple.

Anything with whiskers is off-limits.

Anything with big floppy ears and/or a tail is off-limits.

You might think your cuddly-wuddly stunt is going to get you laid, but think again. You are oozing with neediness.

While women can sometimes be tough to read, there's one thing you can be sure of:

None of them wants to bang a mouse.

THE COSTUME SCALE OF INAPPROPRIATENESS

Gladiator   Viking   Burt Reynolds   Ninja   Cop   Cowboy

APPROPRIATE   **GREY**

Tennis Player   Mouse   Bunny   Raggedy Ann   Winnie the Pooh

AREA   INAPPROPRIATE

★ DON'T BE THAT GUY ★

GUYS WHO WEAR VINTAGE CLOTHES

There were reasons Don Knotts didn't get laid, and you're wearing them.

If it were October 31, I'd say knock your socks off, but it isn't. It's just another day of us all trying to pretend you don't look dumb.

Oh, and before you go bragging about the $4 price tag on that 35-year-old pair of pants, remember it's going to cost twice that much to dry-clean the antique skidmarks from its fibers.

★ DON'T BE THAT GUY ★

GUYS WHO WEAR WINTER HATS INDOORS

You must be pretty chilly, huh? Good thing you got that little wool cap to go over your head.

Quick question: if you're so cold, then why are you sweating? I can see little beads welling up under your cute furry brim.

Wait a second, you're not cold after all. You're warm. Dare I say, uncomfortably warm. You just can't bear to part with how adorable you look in that little beanie.

You will swelter through this entire day just to ensure that your pouty lips are accentuated.

Wow, that's some vain-ass shit.

A FEW MORE FASHION NO-NOS . . .

The Denim Flamingo

Skinny jeans. That magical combination of waifish, feminine calves and the unfathomable desire to showcase them.

Mr. Above-the-Knee Dungaree

When a lack of fashion sense, a lack of decency, and an abundance of NASCAR collide.

The Saggy Ass

A look that says, "I may have lost the ability to walk properly, but at least most of my underpants are showing."

The Faux Pro

The irony of flaunting your love for a favorite player while the XXL mesh flaunts how incredibly unathletic your body is.

Etiquette

★ DON'T BE THAT GUY ★

GUYS WHO OVER-HUG

When I get married, feel free to throw your arms around me.

When I have a child, by all means, wrap me into your chest.

These are milestones that warrant such a gesture of affection.

When I come over for poker, however, don't. Don't you dare.

In fact, here's a list to refer to when you're unsure:

HUG ME	DON'T HUG ME
I return from combat	I spring for lunch
Someone dies	I get a hit in softball
I earn a degree	I get over a cold
I go into surgery	I get blackjack

A GUIDE TO ACCEPTABLE HUGGING ALTERNATIVES

A.

B.

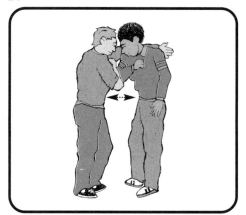

THE FIST BASH A very manly option, provided you don't wince when your knuckles collide.

THE ARM-TUCK HUG Simply placing your arms between you will keep your two warm, male chests from becoming one.

C.

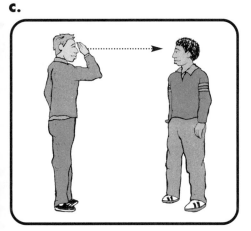

THE SALUTE Military and whimsical, this is an underutilized greeting for saying hello at a distance.

D.

THE FINGER POINT A playful option, but be careful not to turn a simple pointed finger into a fake pistol while making a clicking sound with your mouth. If this happens, just go over and hug the guy.

★ DON'T BE THAT GUY ★

GUYS WHO WON'T ACKNOWLEDGE THEIR LACTOSE INTOLERANCE

When you lay an egg that clears out a room right after you eat a yogurt, you're lactose intolerant and you need to take a pill to correct it.

When you grab a slice, then minutes later see us grabbing our mouths, again, you're lactose intolerant and you need to see a doctor.

You seem to have forgotten that ice cream cones aren't supposed to cause labor-like cramps and sweating. They're supposed to make you smile and giggle.

No more "Sorry, I don't know what's wrong with me" crap. Because I do.

You're lactose intolerant.

So please, show some well-overdue respect for your condition and your friends and lay off the goddamned dairy.

GUYS WHO STRIKE UP CONVERSATIONS AT URINALS

Would it kill you to ride out these sixty seconds in silence?

Personally, my goal in here is simple: to relieve myself and exit before the barn-like stench overcomes me.

Under different circumstances, I'd be more than happy to chat with you—like, for example, when we're not both holding our nude penises.

If the boredom is really getting to you, try playing "Chase the Pube™" around the urinal with your stream—a nice, private way to kill some time. (See illustration on the next page.)

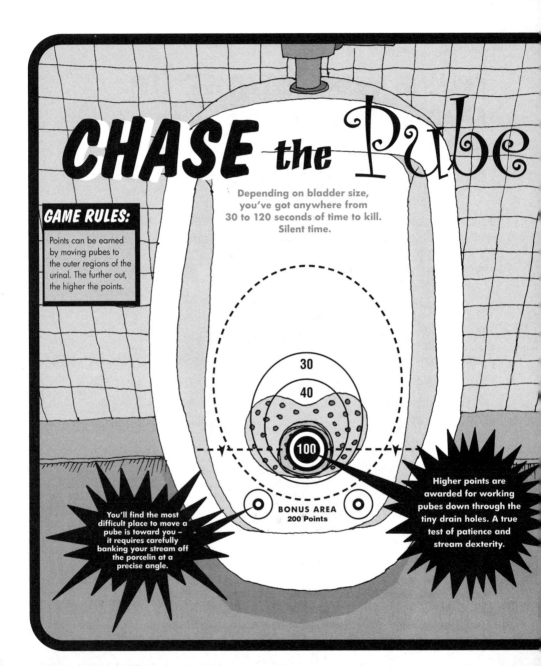

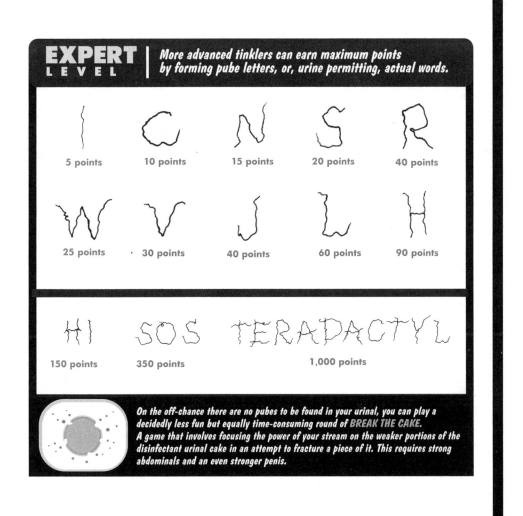

EXPERT
L E V E L

More advanced tinklers can earn maximum points by forming pube letters, or, urine permitting, actual words.

I	C	N	S	R
5 points	10 points	15 points	20 points	40 points
W	V	J	L	H
25 points	30 points	40 points	60 points	90 points

HI	SOS	TERADACTYL
150 points	350 points	1,000 points

On the off-chance there are no pubes to be found in your urinal, you can play a decidedly less fun but equally time-consuming round of BREAK THE CAKE. A game that involves focusing the power of your stream on the weaker portions of the disinfectant urinal cake in an attempt to fracture a piece of it. This requires strong abdominals and an even stronger penis.

★ DON'T BE THAT GUY ★

PRACTICAL JOKE GUYS WHO MISTAKE DANGER FOR HUMOR

Would it be funny if you stuck Krazy glue all over Rick's pillow?

No, it wouldn't, because Rick would probably die.

There's a not-so-fine line between humorous and horrifying that you seem unable to distinguish, otherwise you wouldn't be asking me if you should mail that dead sheep's head to your teacher.

Yet another lighthearted prank I'm going to have to vote no on.

★ DON'T BE THAT GUY ★

GUYS WHO TRY TO GET US TO LOOK AT THEIR GIANT TURDS

Look, we've all birthed a toilet child before. We've all stood back and marveled at our bovine accomplishments. But we did it alone, as the Lord intended.

You've got some gall coming out of the bathroom like that, urging a viewing as if we'd be the weird ones if we turned you down.

Fast forward to what that scene would be like if we actually followed you back in there.

You, standing over the bowl, pointing out measurements and topographical features. And us, peering over your shoulder with kerchiefs over our mouths like rookie detectives at a crime scene trying to suppress our gag reflexes.

Feel free to stay in there as long as you want—poke it, weigh it, photograph it—whatever you're into.

But this is one moment of pride you're going to have to bask in solo.

★ DON'T BE THAT GUY ★

GUYS WHO THINK WE HAVE A SPECIAL HANDSHAKE WHEN WE REALLY DON'T

Don't lay some fist-finger-snap combo on me and expect me to fall in sync with you.

We've never done this before. In fact, you and I barely even shake hands. It's usually just a simple nod or "What's up?"

So what's with the five-finger dance all of a sudden?

Not to discourage your little burst of street flair, but if we're going to pull this off, you really need to walk me through it first. Just because you've been watching *The Wire* doesn't mean the rest of us have.

★ DON'T BE THAT GUY ★

GUYS WHO RUB THEIR FRIENDS' SHOULDERS

Let me be the first to say, this feels really nice. But let me also say, you shouldn't do it anymore.

Yes, your fingers are meaty and strong and, yes, I've been a bit tense lately, but it still doesn't make it right.

Here I am just thinking you're coming over for an innocent high-five, and then *bam!*

It's man-on-man shiatsu time.

While I'm 95% sure you're doing this in a friendship/uncle sort of way, it's that 5% that keeps it from being truly enjoyable . . .

And makes me wonder if you're sniffing my hair while you're back there.

★ DON'T BE THAT GUY ★

OLD GUYS WHO FART AND THINK WE DON'T NOTICE

I believe that you can't hear yourself break wind anymore. I also buy that you've lost the ability to smell how atrocious it is. But you have to know we can see you lift your leg up every time.

All is fair in the haze of geriatric anonymity, but when people under eighty are around and you rip one, everyone knows it.

We hear it. We smell it. We taste it.

Because sadly, the years have not only dulled your senses, they've seasoned your colon to toxic levels.

★ DON'T BE THAT GUY ★

GUYS WHO BRING MORE THAN ONE OTHER GUY TO A PARTY

If this had been an invitation to a pick-up football game, then you'd be a hero right now. But it wasn't, so let's use our heads here.

You've sent this nicely balanced party spiraling into a Code 5 Sausagefest just so you could have a couple of more guys to high-five during the night.

This is the logic of a crazy person.

So let's go ahead and put a two-man capper on all coed soirees from here on in. Not only will you have a better time, you'll greatly reduce your chances of waking up in the arms of another dude.

★ DON'T BE THAT GUY ★

GUYS WHO ACTUALLY THINK THEY DO A GOOD ROBOT

There's a look in your eye that isn't saying, "Hey, isn't this funny?"

It's saying, "Hey, isn't this weirdly machine-like?"

You can't hide what you're feeling. You are mechanical.

Your limbs have steel joints.

Your secret talent has finally been unleashed, right here at this wedding.

Unfortunately, from where we're standing, you look less like a robot and more like an extremely uncoordinated human being.

Possibly with some sort of muscular-system disorder.

★ DON'T BE THAT GUY ★

GUYS WHO TRY TO GET US TO BET ON EVERYTHING

Can you make that shot from your cubicle into the wastebasket?

Probably not.

Do we want to bet $5 on it?

No. No, we don't.

Can you get that girl's number over there?

Maybe.

Do we want to wager a cool Hamilton on it?

Again, no.

Sorry that regular life isn't giving you the rush you're after, but these aren't things we want to watch, let alone bet on.

Honestly, we're dreading the day you have to hitch a ride to work because you lost your car in a game of "guess which hand."

★ DON'T BE THAT GUY ★

GUYS WHO EXPLODE IN PUBLIC BATHROOMS

As men, we're not held to the same code of decency as women, and we should celebrate that.

But not like this.

If the human body is capable of such feats as fighting disease and creating new life, it can certainly control the force with which we poo.

Unless your last meal was at a taqueria in Guadalajara, when you explode on a toilet, it's because you want to.

And while you remain anonymous behind that stall door, I hope you still feel some shame from the fecal concerto you're subjecting us to.

GUYS WHO WEAR SUNGLASSES DURING NONPROFESSIONAL POKER GAMES

In a game where half of us can't remember if a flush beats a full house, what are the chances that your swelling corneas are giving away your bluff?

This isn't Vegas; this is my basement. Hence, the twenty-five-cent blinds and the fact that the woman you saw on your way in was my mom.

It's also kind of infuriating how you keep picking up the wrong colored chips and knocking over your beer because you can't see.

So how about you take those things off, thank my mom for the Hot Pockets she just brought downstairs, and we can all get back to winning less than a dollar off each other?

BARS, Drinking & ENTERTAINMENT

GUYS WHO TRY TO TURN EVERY ACTIVITY INTO A DRINKING ACTIVITY

Catching a buzz before we head to the museum doesn't sound like a good idea at all.

Throwing back a few before our bike ride sounds like an even worse one.

I'm not sure what added enjoyment you glean from these events by being pickled, but I am sure about one thing.

Somebody's an alcoholic.

GUYS IN BARS WHO PRETEND THEY'RE READING

The jig's up, fellas. We know you're not really reading.

You can't be; it's too dark.

It is light enough, however, to see you looking up to make sure people see you "reading."

If you think literature is a big hook with women, then maybe you should try talking to a girl about a book instead of reading one in front of her.

Clearly, there are better ways to exude the intellectual vibe without bringing props with you, or at least places where you won't look like you're trying so hard.

Like the library. Or France.

GUYS WHO PRETEND THEY'RE HAVING A LOT MORE FUN THAN THEY REALLY ARE

So you're the fun guy.

The one everyone in your crew counts on to keep things festive.

The guy who needs no direct stimulus to warrant any number of inappropriate outbursts.

Painful classics like "Boo-yah!" and "Let's do this!"

Nothing happened to justify this enthusiasm. There's no game on TV, and by the looks of things, none of your friends said anything all that exciting.

You're having a very mediocre time.

You know it and we know it.

★ DON'T BE THAT GUY ★

GUYS WHO DODGE PAYING FOR THEIR ROUND OF DRINKS

We know that's not a real cell phone conversation you're having. Your phone didn't ring, vibrate, or light up.

We're also very aware of your conveniently timed trips to the bathroom and nonchalant drifts over to the jukebox when your round is up.

You're as transparent as your friends' empty glasses.

And honestly, how many times do you think you can get away with your famous "Shit, they don't take credit cards here?" schtick.

Your pettiness is undermining the entire Round System as we know it.

So before you throw the entire thing off, why not go ahead and pony up for a round?

It's a small price to pay for friendship.

★ DON'T BE THAT GUY ★

GUYS WHO IMPERSONATE ARNOLD SCHWARZENEGGER

Everyone loves a good impression.

Everyone hates a guy who impersonates Arnold.

Why? Because it takes no skill.

It is hands down the easiest impression on the face of the earth.

My seven-year-old nephew does a good Arnold.

My mom does a good Arnold.

So do everyone a favor and drop the *Aaanuld*.

You'll be amazed at how much more everyone likes you.

A SAMPLING OF ARNOLD IMPRESSIONISTS

A-HOLES WHO WORK THE DOORS AT CLUBS

To all you Vin Diesel–looking, fake earpiece–wearing, power-trip dickheads, shamelessly ignoring hundreds of guys every night—just know this:

Someday you're going to be on the other side of that enchanted velvet rope, and unless you've got a pair of double D's hidden underneath that Armani T-shirt, you might want to grab a magazine. It's going to be awhile.

GUYS IN VEGAS WHO INSIST ON GAMBLING DESPITE BEING PLASTERED

It's 4:00 a.m. Your shirt is damp and there's a schmear of glitter across your forehead. You stumble to a blackjack table and slap down a wad of crumpled cash, a mint, some loose tobacco, and a rubber. You order a White Russian from a passing waitress, who turns out to be, in fact, not a waitress, or an employee of the casino, or a woman. You then proceed to treat your tablemates to a mind-boggling exposé of math, strategy, and fine sensory motor skills, some highlights of which include: pensively staring at eighteens deciding if you should take a card, making hand gestures that resemble neither "hit" nor "stay," and providing a spirited commentary on the dealer's hand—"That is fucking bullshit . . . Juan! Fucking nineteen, you cocksucker!"

As for us, well, in addition to dealer blackjack, we're forced to add "getting vomited on" to our list of fears for the evening.

★ DON'T BE THAT GUY ★

BARBACKS WHO STAND AROUND WHILE WE NEED DRINKS

Are you absolutely sure you can't get us a drink? Because you look perfectly qualified.

You also look like you've got some time on your hands, because you're just standing there looking at us.

If the answer is definitely no, then could you do us all a favor and not dress exactly like the bartenders?

Put on an orange vest or something, because right now we want to pound on you.

GUYS WHO STILL QUOTE THE HOLY GRAIL AND/OR SPINAL TAP

Like you, I enjoyed these movies very much. And, like you, I've seen several hundred movies since then.

Which begs the question that surely some shred of dialogue between the early 1980s and now is worthy of replacing "This one goes to eleven."

Some actor between when Ford was president and now must have said something funnier than "It's only a flesh wound."

If you were paying attention, you'd notice that as the years have passed, people laugh less every time you use these lines.

Even with your cute British accent.

THE MOVIE MONOLOGIST: A close cousin to the movie quoter is the movie monologist. The guy who at any given moment will throw down a two- to five-minute soliloquy from one of his favorite films, regardless of whether or not we want to hear it. Perhaps this section will help him to understand that every time he gives one of his famous monologues, we're giving one too. In our heads.

"The path of the righteous man is beset on all sides by the inequities of the selfish and the tyranny of evil men. Blessed is he who, in the name of charity and good will, shepherds the weak through the valley of darkness, for he is truly his brother's keeper and the finder of lost children and I will strike down upon thee with great vengeance and furious anger those who attempt to poison and destroy my brothers. And you will know my name is the Lord when I lay my vengeance upon you..."

★ DON'T BE THAT GUY ★

GUYS WHO ALWAYS HAVE A NEW SHITTY BAND FOR US TO LISTEN TO

Have I heard of the Gracious Baboons?

No, I can't say that I have, but I'm sure you have a CD of theirs you want me to listen to.

What joy do you take in scouring the nether regions of the music industry for the most obscure garbage out there?

You're 0 for 20 so far, so why don't we take a break from all this nonsense and listen to some Billy Joel for awhile?

GUYS WHO LISTEN TO DAVE MATTHEWS ON PURPOSE

It's one thing to get caught off guard with the radio on and find yourself busting out a little falsetto during "Satellite."

It's another thing entirely when you're listening to him by choice.

Honestly, even Dave Matthews would think that's weird.

His music is very specifically written for women. His lyrics are for women. His melodies are for women.

Young women with budding breasts and SATs to study for.

THE TOP FIVE DAVE MATTHEWS LYRICS
YOU DON'T WANT TO
GET CAUGHT SINGING OUT LOUD

If you come upon these particular sections, it is strongly advised that you hum until things get less awkward.

Always

I wish that I could climb inside your mind
And spend some time and hug and hold you.

Crash into Me

And I come into you
And I come into you

Lover Lay Down

Kiss me oh won't you kiss me now
And sleep I would inside your mouth

Crush

Lovely lady, let me drink you, please.
Won't spill a drop, no, I promise you.

I Did It

I'm mixing up a bunch of magic stuff
A magic mushroom cloud of care

GUYS WHO DANCE WITH THE GIRLS DANCING ON THE BAR

I'm curious what your next move is . . . to walk in on me while I'm watching a porno?

What makes you think we want to see you with your hat on sideways, smack dab in the middle of our fantasy?

Just one rotation of your cabbage-patch has sent a ripple of flaccidity through this entire club.

These girls were kind enough to provide us with some masturbatory fodder and your skinny Eminem ass just killed it.

THE DON'T BE THAT GUY
FINAL EXAM

Now it's time to scan back through the book and tally up the number of guys who reminded you of you. Next, match that number with the chart to the right for a highly scientific assessment of how your life is going.

YES ANSWERS	HOW SCREWED YOU ARE
◯ 0	Go back through the book again, this time without lying.
◯ 1-4	You're in decent shape. Chances are more people like you than hate you, which is nice.
◯ 5-8	You're on the cusp of being very unlikable. It's time to nip these things in the bud before your friends start dropping like flies.
◯ 9-12	You're very difficult to be around. When you show up places to meet friends, you get the recurring feeling that they were just talking about you. Then you ask them and they tell you they were.
◯ 13-16	You're curious why you don't date much. And why a lot of people tell you to "go fuck yourself."
◯ 17+	Thinking back, you can't remember the last time you enjoyed being with yourself.

Colin Nissan
Writer

Colin Nissan is a freelance advertising copywriter living in Brooklyn, New York. He is also a guy, a gender that has provided him with two things: one, an alarming amount of body hair. And two, the ability to perceive highly unflattering insights into his own kind. Insights that have all been compiled into one book, which will likely destroy most of his friendships. Some of Colin's less hurtful writing can be found on McSweeney's Internet Tendency, among other places.

Email Colin - colin@dontbethatguybook.com

Sean Farrell
Illustrator

Sean Farrell is a freelance advertising art director living in San Francisco. Sean enjoys many art forms, such as drawing and painting. His initial idea was to sculpt the guys in this book. While ambitious, this idea was also very dumb. Thankfully, he was able to sell his new kiln on eBay and buy some pens. Some of Sean's other handiwork can be seen in his line of greeting cards, Bald Guy Greetings.

Email Sean - sean@dontbethatguybook.com

*For all the guys
who helped inspire this book*

Dr. Bucinskas, Darryl Nissan, Joe Nissan, Kevin Garrelick, David Franks, Jon Franks, Billy Hoover, Mike McGuirk, Dr. Brazelton, Jeff Walker, Mark Cassetta, John Sangiovanni, Kevin Tobin, Orin Shakerdge, Omer Oleibovich, Jason Nissan, Neil Nissan, Brian Nissan, Emile Nissan, Corey Sturmfels, Rennie Zettel, Ian McCallister, Kevin Whiffin, Skye Ellis, Tim Gibson, Rodney Coleman, Brian Roberts, Goob, Tommy Cullinane, Eric Deehan, Steve Murphy, Gary Gailius, Adam Kanner, Eddie MacLean, Chris Mee, Doug Williamson, Mike Pina, Rob Shields, Lee Stephens, Brad Thome, Dean Lewis, Phil Hillman, Damien Cave, Brian Gray, Steve Briggs, Joey Curtis, Lee Gustafson, Harold Kobakoff, Dan O'Donnell, Allan Duncan, Seth Bruning, Rob Foster, Brian Duffy, Alon Friedman, Kevin Green, Moogie Klingman, Chris Leps, Ben Meth, Dan Meth, Paul Schauder, Steve Shakerdge, Dave Swartz, Pete Brophy, Dave Freeland, Chris Michalopoulos, Robbie McCormick, Dr. O'Malley, Matt Baker, Tim Igo, Kevin Clarke, Alfredo Chang, Murad Abed, Ronan Abed, Rob Cathcart, Duffy McNulty, Matt Webster, Jeff Hickey, Kurt Cooney, Brian Goodwin, Dimitri Coats, Greg Luconi, John O'Neil, Mike Benjamin, Kenny Lefebvre, Ben Reznikoff, Elliot Baker, Corey O'Brien, Frank Pappa, Palmucci, Bill Somes, Stu Berkowitz, Thanh Diec, Doug Heffernan, Mr. Wong, Mike Nadler, Jeff Maron, Mr. Dutton, Joe Delory, Mr. Walton, John Harney, Nathaniel Kessler, Luke Gallager, Dave Platte, Nicky Bruning, Dennis Fuccione, Vinnie Best, Matt Vescovo, Joe Leone, Joseph Fury, Francisco Castro, Ernesto Suarez, Todd Washburn, Craig Mangan, Sean Finucane, Dave Pesko, Freddy Underwood, Mike Sweeney, Alex "Grossdog" Grossman, Peter North, Jamie Harrington, George Mallett, Billy Konrad, Brant Chamberlain, Steven Chamberlain, Bob Chamberlain, Tucker Sferro, Bill Sferro, Scott Wicombe, Scott "Fart n' smelly" Martinelli, Keith Lavangie, Ryan Lavangie, the Davis Brothers, Pat "Sully" Sullivan, John Barnett, Dick Bernard, Bobby Connelly, Geremy Alosa, Eric "Iroc" Ritcey, Chad Chambers, Dave Morin, Mike Kelly, Mike "Momo" Molinari, Ted Collette, Byron Fisher, Mike Pescatore, Greg Bellerose, Jeff Bellerose, Jeff Soares, Jebidiah Soares, Owen Monroe, Keith Norton, Kevin Murphy, Jim Amadeo, Scott Lanier, Mack Fitzgerald, Marty Anderson, Brian McDevitt, Ace, Pete Afanasiw, Tom Bixby, Peter Brown, Patrick Brennan, Jeff Brennan, Bruce Bradford, Mike Chamberlain, Rob Cheesman, Chris Clemens, Mike Connors, Duncan Frazee, Timmy "Timma" Golden, Derek Holte, Raymond Hayes, Sean Shea, Jeff Timperi, Demetri Souretis, Tom Steel, Mark and Randy Trongone, Steven Studley, Derek Fillon, Jeff Goodby, Rich Silverstein, Paul Venables, Greg Bell, Dan Rollman, Ian Kalman, Mark Wenneker, Dave Laden, Matt Smukler, Noam Murro, Chris Smith, Joel Clement, Andy McKeon, Steve Dildarian, David Martinelli, Jack Woodworth, Johnny Mower, Terry Finley, Carl Litchefield, Brian McPherson, Ben Kincaid, Brendan Keenan, Christopher Gyorgy, Colin Probert, Eben Carr, Harry Cocciolo, Marty Wenzell, Lionel Carreon, John Nussbaum, James Horner, Matt Rivitz, Tyler Magnusson, Michael Kennedy, Steve Simpson, Al Kelly, Payo, Todd Grant, Jon Soto, Tom Miller, Jeremy Postaer, Lawson Clarke, Penn Clarke, Terry Clarke, Spencer Deadrick, Gerry Graf, Steve Luker, Greg Harrison, Goldy, Eivand Uland, Roy Ward, Ken Pearlman, Dominic Farrell, Richard Donnelly, Jimmy Farrell, Jimmy Farrell Jr., Chris Moore, Jeffrey Moore, Jimmy McLaughlin, Johnny McLaughlin, Matt Bijarchi, Larry Goldstein, Rick Jagelski, Peter Brown, Terry Yaffee, Bobby Long, Paul Mahoney, Luke Short, Wayne Carney, Chris Beresford Hill, Mark Rurka, William Huber, Russ Quackenbush, Joey Lepere, Matt Bunzel, Brian Hayes, Steven Carver, Claude Shade, Steven Barry, Mike West, John McIntire, Mike McIntire, Dan Saro, Kevin Begley, Steve Connelly, Sean Whelan.

Jimmy Finucane, Chris Decarlo, Devin the Dude, Peter Scott, Michael Gabriel, Zach Canfield, Bobby Pearce, Jason Ellis, Joe Rose, Jim Dougherty, Jason Ellis, Paul Hirsche, Josh Denberg, Bob Morrow, Greg Reillly, Seth Weisfeld, Ronny Northrop, George Goetz, Al Pavlov, Dennis Zanetti, Jason Geddis, Matt Taylor, Brett Berlin, Ben Posadlo, Charles Baker, Ricky Mullins, James Alvord, Rick Russell, Dan Garrelick, Mike Norton, Tom Kelly, Steve MacGuire, John Spooner, Jun Diaz, Matt Kelly, Ian Reichenthal, Alex McMaster, Dan Levine, Mike Weitzen, Chris Miagi, Fred & Farid, Bob Molineaux, Torres, Bobby McCourt, Macho, Mike Lawson, Mike Echel, Brian Driscoll, Cory Noonan, Jon Metters, Bryan Norman, Edward Boches, Jim Elliot, Ted Jendrysik, Dan Felgner, Scott Gutterson, Fuzz, Nick Boynton, John Pearse, Mark Waldek, Fran Gurdy, Tom Esch, Bobby McCue, Kevin Miller, Jeff Terry, Eric Haya, Dave Gray, Scott Forsberg, Jerry Ruzeki, Sean Miller, John Mulvany, Fitz, John Birmingham, Derek Benbow, Edgar, Jason Biggerstaff, Mark Undercoffler, Steve Brown, Otis Coo, Steve Millhouse, Brian Friedrich, Robert Riccardi, Pearl Washington, Pat Brown, Riker, Rafi Kugler, Tony Saxe, Jason Ellis, Taylor Bryant, Bilba, Mike Maguire, Ray Hayes, Tim McMahon, Jesse Golden, Steve Fleming, Paul Mahoney, Macka, Scott McIntire, Brian Mealey, Bob Mealey, Jody Scannel, Liam Skully, Mike Webber, Thad Baker, Steve Cram, Steve Daugherty, Rob Rich, Kevin Rhodes, Tom Routson, Max Fallon, Todd Puckett, Sean Ehringer, Todd Grantham, Michael Stock, Dan Southwick, Noah Dasho, Michael Gabriel, Robert Cribley, Will Hung, Scott Vitrone, Dennis O'Donnell, Charlie Boyle, James English, Merv Rey, Han Lin, Yo Umeda, Mikey Holte, Bobby Manning, Mike Manning, Oskar Kelly